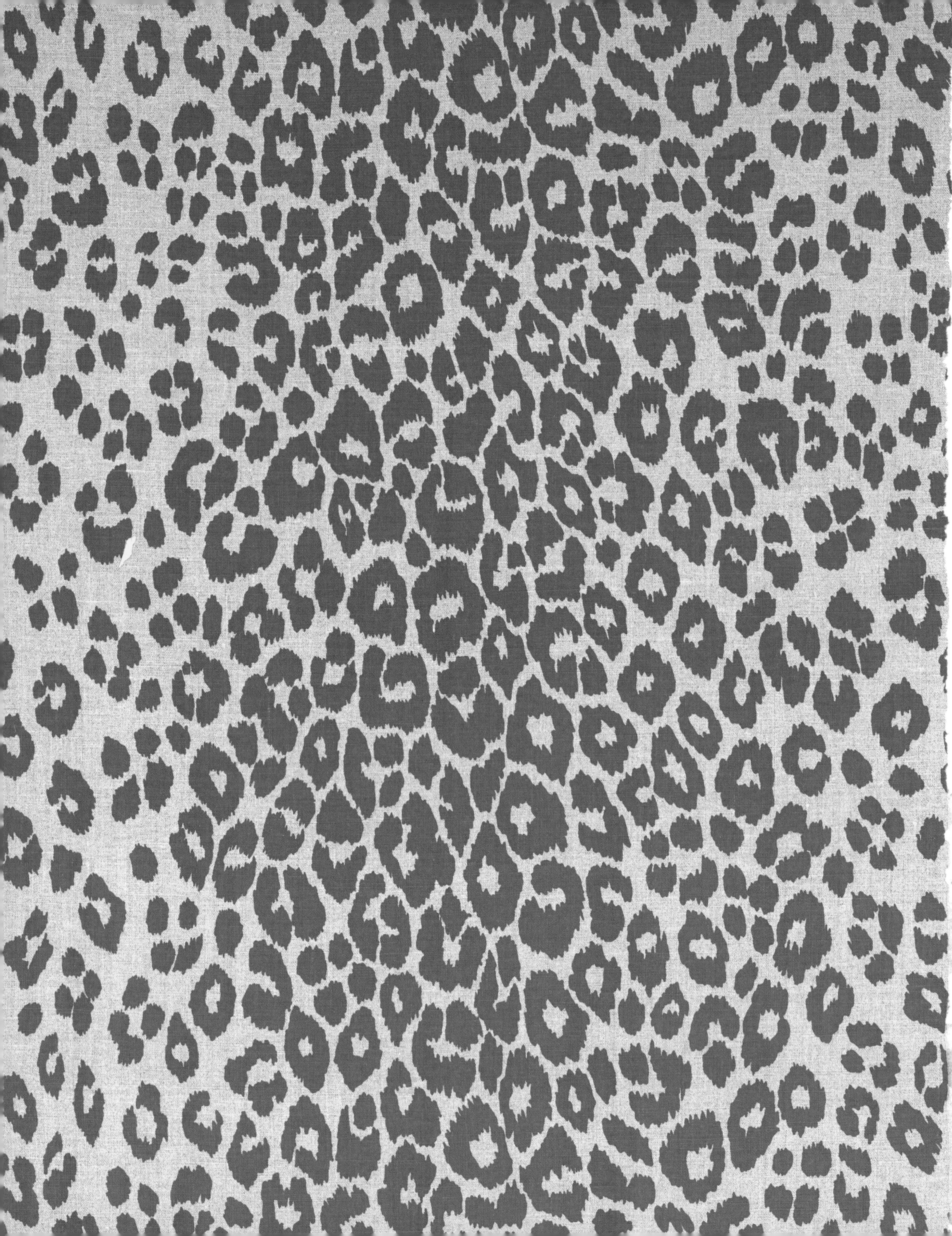

# MORE *is* MORE *is* MORE

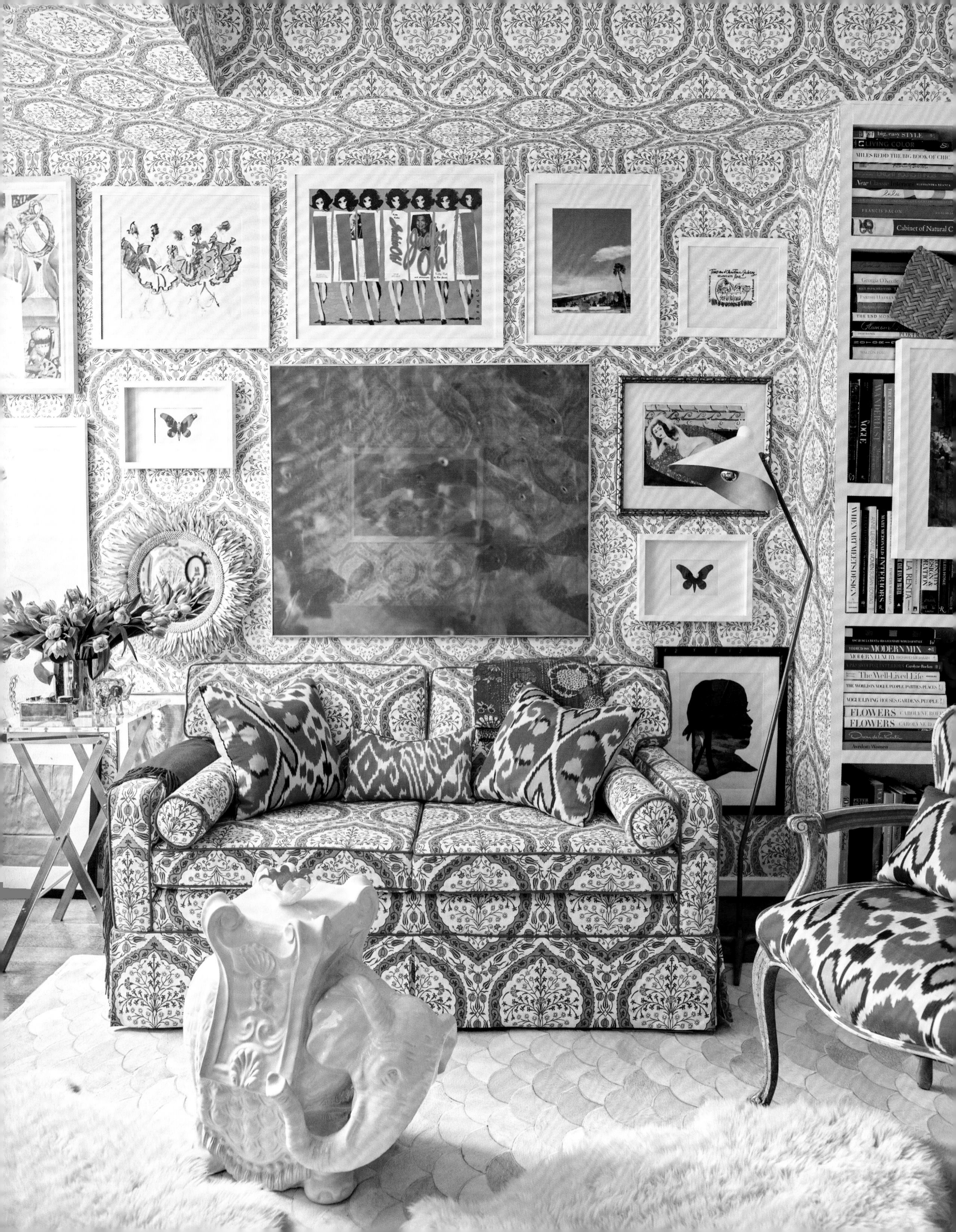
big, easy STYLE
LIVING COLOR
MILES REDD THE BIG BOOK OF CHIC
FRANCIS BACON
Cabinet of Natural C
Georgia O'Keeffe
THE END
MODERN MIX
MODERN LUXURY
The Well-Lived Life
THE WORLD IN VOGUE PEOPLE PARTIES PLACES
VOGUE LIVING HOUSES, GARDENS, PEOPLE
FLOWERS
FLOWERS
Avedon: Women
LA RENTA
INTERIORS

# MORE *is* MORE *is* MORE

## TODAY'S MAXIMALIST INTERIORS

CARL DELLATORE

Foreword by **DARA CAPONIGRO**

RIZZOLI
NEW YORK
New York · Paris · London · Milan

# CONTENTS



STEPHEN DIGERONIMO ▲

MICHELLE NUSSBAUMER ▶

# FOREWORD

LET'S START WITH A LOVE STORY. ONE DAY IN THE 1980S, when I was an impressionable young shelter-magazine editor in my twenties, I went to a press preview and fell head over heels for a wallpaper that was pretty out of character for me, an avowed minimalist even then. It had a bright lemon-yellow ground and an aubergine damask motif emblazoned all over it, and all I can say is that it beckoned to me with the promise of a life different from the one my pared-down, under-the-radar sensibility seemed to have in store for me: splashy, statement-making, unapologetically au courant. It was the '80s, after all. So I scrimped and saved until I could finally afford to go out and buy it. I even hired a decorative painter to stipple the trim in a matching eggplant color. My fling with flashy was about to take wing.

Well, the bloom took two seconds to fade off that rose. The minute the wallpaper went up, the soundtrack to my so-called new look came to a screeching halt, and I started wondering how long I would have to save until I could afford to take it down. The moral of this story is twofold: First, as a confirmed minimalist writing the foreword to a book called *More Is More Is More*, I want to provide full disclosure. Maximalism, in all its vivid, lacquer-splashed, pattern-on-pattern euphoria, gives me great joy and has served me well as a former magazine editor and the current creative director of legendary design house Schumacher, but these days I mostly respect it as an enthusiastic admirer and observer. One of the things I love so much about being an editor and a design creative is the ability it gives me to channel so many different parts of my personality. It's clear that Carl Dellatore delights in the same vantage point, and as the sheer joie de vivre barely contained within these pages proves, it is a privileged perch indeed. You'll be hard-pressed to find more jubilance between two pieces of clothbound cardboard—or anywhere else for that matter. There is just so much to love here.

The other moral of my story, borne out by a career that has kept me abreast of every trend, tendency, and ripple the decorative arts have been through over the years, is that the bar-none, number one, ultimate truth about good decorating, no matter where you stand on the style spectrum, is that it *has* to make you fall in love. Even if it's a leap of faith (or out of character).

A common misconception about rooms that are "a lot" is that someone just threw everything and the kitchen sink at them and waited to see what would stick. Interiors with plenty of bells and whistles can feel offhand and deliciously thrown together—in fact, the very best of them do—but I assure you nothing could be further from the truth. It takes an expertise bordering on genius to craft that kind of magic, and the projects Dellatore has pulled together here truly dazzle. From Summer Thornton and Martyn Lawrence Bullard to Bunny Williams and Redd Kaihoi, these are practitioners at the very top of their game, doing what they do best: mixing paisleys with arabesques and *indiennes* and ticking-stripe ruffles in a dining nook that charms; layering stripes atop animal prints amid a sea of fringe in a serene shell-pink bedroom; perfectly calibrating gilt antiques and top-notch art in a living room scheme that feels impossibly, counterintuitively unfussy; combining

trompe l'oeil, velvet, and rippling carved wood into a swoony fantasia that completely sweeps you away. This is nothing less than a master class in how to properly gild the lily. Want to learn how to live out loud? Like, really, really sing? Look no further.

Eminently one-of-a-kind, these are confident, exuberant, extroverted interiors that demand an audience. No prisoners. No regrets. These spaces want to be lived in, laughed in, cried in, loved in. They make you feel the way you feel when you dress up for a party, look at yourself in the mirror, and know you nailed it. They are the perfect backdrop for intrigues, dramas, comedies of errors, and, yes, romances. Speaking as an arbiter on the other end of the spectrum, I can tell you this: the world would be a boring, sad place without them. Go ahead and take a look. I dare you not to fall in love.



Dara Caponigro
Creative director, Schumacher
Editor-in-chief, *Frederic*

**KELLY BEHUN**

"For me, the mash-up of patterns works here because we kept to a consistent blue-and-white palette and mixed the strict geometry of the chevron-patterned wallpaper with the looser, more organic shapes in the hand-knotted Moroccan rug. Side by side, they actually harmonize with each other instead of competing."

**PHILIP MITCHELL**

"A successful grouping for a gallery wall should not match but be composed of varying pieces of different scale, colors, mediums, and styles that have a common thread that ties them all together. This will create contrast, a visual flow, and, most importantly, a unique and personal point of view for the collection."

TECTURE OF CHARLES A. PLATT
ACANTHUS PRESS
SCHAFER III

WHAT DEFINES MAXIMALISM? IN THE DESIGN WORLD, opinions vary greatly. There is one faction that says a level of excess is pivotal. Some suggest that unexpected, often shocking color (or color combinations) should take center stage. Still others believe a mix of patterns to be de rigueur. The list goes on.

As most views about design are ultimately subjective, they are all correct. But no matter its form, maximalism has been with us as long as the decorative arts. At the turn of the twentieth century, the Breakers, Richard Morris Hunt's dichotomous seventy-room "cottage" designed for the Vanderbilt family and decorated by the team of Jules Allard and Sons and Ogden Codman Jr., defined Gilded Age maximalism through the use of architectural elements. No expense was spared toward cementing an aura of supreme wealth and status: lavish marbles from Italy, exotic woods and chromatic tiles from far-flung locales, and a stupendous mantel from a French château shipped at great expense for the Breakers library.

Fast-forward to the 1960s and '70s, when Manhattan society lauded Robert Denning and Vincent Fourcade's supremely layered rooms focused on opulent furnishings, with every surface adorned: high-gloss lacquered walls, silk damask settees, neo-baroque curtains, delicately pleated custom lampshades, and dyed-to-match passementerie. Their work was described by *Architectural Digest*'s Mitchell Owens as "magnificent excess" for clients as varied as Henry Kissinger and Oscar de la Renta.

And then there is the present-day decorator Kelly Wearstler's twenty-first-century maximalism—an interpretation of old Hollywood glamour, conjured not through excess but with grand-scaled patterns, inventive silhouettes, audacious color, and her reverence for all things naturalistic, seeing Mother Nature as the ultimate source of inspiration.

There is one quality all these incarnations of maximalist design have in common: *There must be an element of surprise.* Maximalist interiors always create a certain frisson, a sense of amazement, a gleeful jolt for the visitor. When you enter a maximalist room, the question remains, How did the designer ever think of that? To achieve surprise, creativity is a necessity.

Creativity in the decorative arts is expressed in the ability to think outside the oft-clichéd box—to be imaginative, to celebrate curiosity, and to come up with original ideas. It's the creation of spaces that eclipse the predictable. The ways you'll find designers expressing their creativity in this book fall into five categories, or chapters: color, elements, pattern, layering, and surfaces.

You'll find an otherwise austere Manhattan entryway lacquered floor to ceiling in several shades of apple green. There's a dizzying array of patterns in a Victorian bedroom unified by botanical motifs. You'll find a carpet woven in an oversize, pixelated garden scene gracing a dining room floor. There's a visually kinetic black-and-white folding screen in a Palm Springs bedroom. And there are rooms with often discordant objects, layered to perfection through a designer's vision.

While I'm on the subject of designer vision, it's important to note that while maximalist interiors often appear busy at first glance, there's always a wealth of knowledge and experience that

SOTTSASS
PORTRAITS OF THE NEW ARCHITECTURE
JAMES TURRELL
THE WORLD ATLAS OF TATTOO
VREELAND MEMOS
VERSACE/AVEDON
FALLINGWATER
Interview
The Economist

serve as the underpinnings in visually demonstrative spaces. Designers know there is a difference between curated and cluttered rooms.

For example, interior designers understand the subtle ways to link the objects in a room to form a narrative, telling a story as the eye lands on each element and then moves to the next. An understanding of color theory is key, as when pairing complementary hues—burnished terracotta balanced by just the right shade of teal. And of course, there's the interplay of silhouettes, with a feminine, curvaceous chair juxtaposed against the ridged angles of a Jean-Michel Frank sofa.

Maximalism as a design movement is very much in vogue. Perhaps it's our twenty-first-century wish to feel bright and celebratory; perhaps it's the antidote to decades of midcentury-inflected minimalism; or perhaps it's the influence of social media platforms, specifically Instagram.

As a lifelong student of design, I'm always curious to learn the "why" behind the choices made in crafting maximalist interiors. That brings me to the final component of this book: insight from the designers. I've interviewed the designers for each image in this book, writing the captions in close consultation with them to share their process for achieving the marvelously alchemical success of each space. Through their words, you will see each room and gain insight into their aesthetic vision. From these words and images, you will be able to channel their knowledge as thrilling inspiration for the decoration of your own home. As imitation is the sincerest form of flattery, please borrow some ideas from this book. I know I intend to!



**PATRICK MELE**

"As the great Diana Vreeland so succinctly summed up, 'Red is the great clarifier—bright, cleansing, revealing. It makes all colors beautiful.' I am so with Mrs. Vreeland! Red not only makes all colors beautiful, it makes all people beautiful. Red is bold, it is sexy, it is warm and rapturous. Red is declarative and certain; it is the color of life and love. All of these traits together make red the most maximal of colors."

**BRADFORD SHELLHAMMER**

"I knew I wanted Womb chairs to relax and read in while looking out at the Hudson River, and I agonized over the color. Yves Klein blue is just one of those perfect shades. It is as unique as the chairs. The black walls and ceiling provide balance and create a room that is bold but inviting."

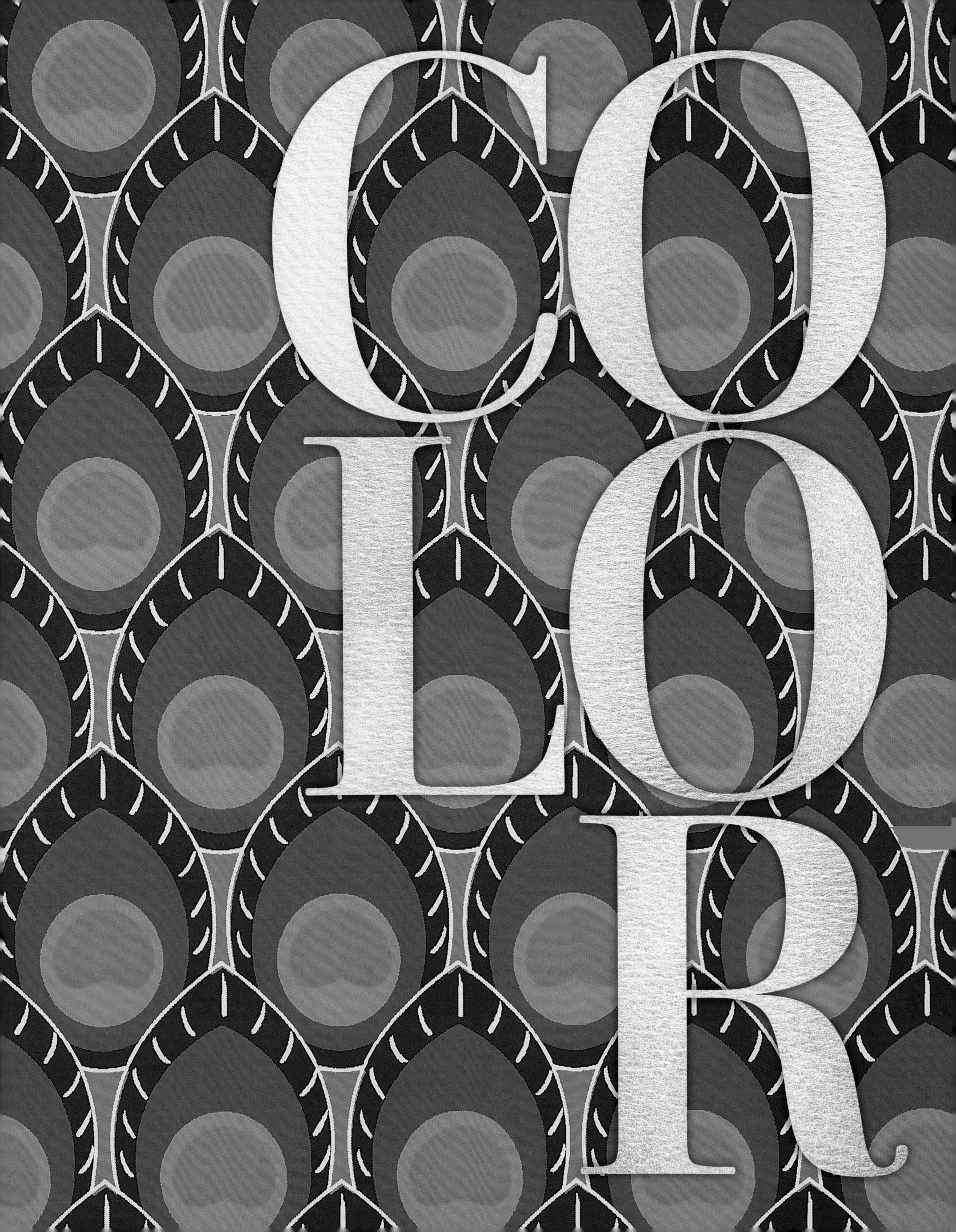
COLOR

LUSH COLOR IS THE KEY TO MAXIMALISM, AS IS A willingness to split with established color theory. And don't forget to add in an unbridled dose of creativity. Along with pattern and silhouette, color makes up the triad of the foundational elements in maximalist design. One might argue that color is the most important of the three.

Historically speaking, there are countless design luminaries who understood and employed a rich, maximalist approach to color in their work. Perhaps the best example is high-society designer Dorothy Draper and her landmark decoration of the Greenbrier hotel in White Sulphur Springs, West Virginia. Her brazen use of green, juxtaposed against red, reinvented a color combination that was once relegated to the end-of-year holiday season. And let's not forget the boisterous mix of shades she conjured for each of the Greenbrier's bedroom suites: yellow curtains against pink ceilings against red upholstery against teal-striped walls, plus riotous floral bedspreads for good measure!

And it's impossible not to remember Billy Baldwin's decoration of legendary fashion editor Diana Vreeland's living room, affectionately dubbed the "garden in hell." Published in *Architectural Digest* in the September/October 1975 issue, the crimson-clad salon, with its floral chintz–lined walls and matching curtains, most certainly set a few dinner-party conversations ablaze with its unabashed flair.

Other notable rooms with a maximalist approach to color include Albert Hadley's legendary brass-lined oxblood library for Brooke Astor with its iconic La Portugaise chintz upholstery; Virginia-born tastemaker Nancy Lancaster's drawing room on London's Avery Row, with its walls sheathed in her famous "buttah-yellah" shade of yellow paint and festooned with corn-silk curtains; and Mark Hampton's brownish black–walled library for Sue and Haydn Cutler, in Fort Worth, Texas, set off in sharp contrast by crisp white furniture and a neutral sisal rug. Even today, these rooms look bold and eye-catching. It's obvious why they've earned a place in the annals of color-referenced design history.

Today, as a culture we've pivoted to the eye-popping, kaleidoscopic, color-rich spaces that define contemporary maximalism. This all invites the question, How do I incorporate maximalist color in my home?

Esteemed interior designer Robert Couturier once told me, "I think the basics about color are like grammar: You need to learn it; you need to absorb it. And then you need to forget it. Taking risks with choosing color is key."

Taking risks, indeed. As you turn the pages to enjoy the many glorious rooms included in this chapter, you will see designers pushing the limits with color, such as a living room inventively striped in vertical bands of progressive hues, drawing your eye around the space, or a room lacquered in a rich marine blue set off by a mix of eggplant-purple and lime-green furniture. Taking risks with assertive color creates one-of-a-kind spaces that catch the eye and delight the visitor.

How do you know if you've landed on the best color, or color combination? I respectfully defer to the aforementioned Dorothy Draper, who famously said, "If it looks right, it is right!"

STEVEN GAMBREL

Previous spread: "The library of this Manhattan apartment draws its inspiration from a world-renowned cocktail lounge in London. Rich velvet, woven horsehair, and a lush silk shag carpet add layers of texture, but it's the unexpected color that defines the space. Paneled walls, lacquered in high-gloss royal purple, are balanced against a vibrant red ceiling. The highly reflective surfaces catch the afternoon light, creating a dynamic, club-like feeling that captures the old-world glamour we were going for."

Right: "For this one-of-a-kind kitchen in an elegantly detailed home just outside Chicago, I chose handmade glass tiles in aquamarine, interspersed with jade tiles, to cover the ceiling and walls. The glass cabinetry and center island are in the same shade of blue and trimmed in polished nickel. The custom range and hood were enameled in forest green. Fumed and ebonized oak floors, set in an Escher-like pattern, serve as a counterpoint. The colors and patterns create a kitchen that's at once monumental, memorable, and supremely inviting."

BRADFORD SHELLHAMMER

"This music room houses a collection of 500 vinyl records. As a result, the art on the walls—vintage posters of Grace Jones, Erasure, Elton John, and other artists—dictated the color choice: loud! I built the room around the art and wall color, loading gray Herman Miller sofas with pillows covered in Marimekko fabrics. This room is meant to be enjoyed with a glass of red wine while listening to music; its color and patterns make it perfect camouflage for that occasional wine spill."

SANDRA BERNHARD
"...INGENIOUS AND UNSETTLING"
WITHOUT YOU I'M NOTHING
CUSU ENTS – CAMBRIDGE CITY COUNCIL – CVG
PRESENT
erasure
+ SUPPORT
+ SPIRIT WALK
LIVE AT THE CAMBRIDGE CORN EXCHANGE
ON SUNDAY JUNE 14 DOORS OPEN AT 8PM
TICKETS AT £6 IN ADVANCE FROM THE BOX OFFICE
ALL PROCEEDS TO INTERNATIONAL AIDS DAY

CYNDI LAUPER
TRUE COLORS
Cyndi Lauper
erasure
THE INNOCENTS IN CONCERT '88
18.5. Berlin – Metropol
BEACON THEATRE
NT SIZE PKGS.
Eero Aarnio
NEUTRA
AMMO

NEW YORK DECO

JEAN DUBUFFET EIN LEBEN IM LAUFSCHRITT
TASCHEN's LONDON

JOHN B. MURRAY

**NICK OLSEN**

Previous spread: “The antique Sultanabad carpet in this room was the first piece we bought, due to its unique blue-and–acid green color palette. I used the most saturated versions of these colors for the blue-lacquered walls and green French chair. The rich plum of the sofa also comes from the carpet, and this velvet tempers the more intense colors in the room, as do healthy doses of black and white.”

Overleaf: “This peacock-blue library doesn’t get much natural light. I chose the color from the adjacent living room’s Ghiordes rug, with the paler version seen in the living room’s silk faille curtains. The oil glaze on the library’s walls, trim, and bookcases reflects light and gives a glamorous, clubby feeling. An intense pop of orange on the throw pillows echoes the persimmon walls beyond.”

**MATTHEW MONROE BEES**

“Lush spring green provides the backdrop for a desk tucked into a corner of the primary bedroom of this Charleston, South Carolina, home. Treating the walls and moldings in the same color creates an enveloping environment, while the trompe l’oeil ‘cornice’ above the door adds a bit of whimsy. The blue-and-white porcelain throughout references the colors in the painting by Lori Glavin.”

JOHN ADAMS

Georgia O'Keeffe ABSTRACTION
Morocco

KEN FULK



Right: "This secret green room is accessed through a doorway hidden in a built-in bookcase at the Battery, a club and boutique hotel in San Francisco. The glossy lacquered walls are the main character of the room, and a big one at that. We chose this hue for its reference to the felt of a poker table, since the speakeasy nature of a hidden room called to mind clandestine card games and deals in the making."

Overleaf: "The peacock-blue walls in this formal dining room required twenty coats of lacquer applied by the talented Willem Racké to mimic the ever-changing shades of San Francisco Bay just outside the window; the view is a real showstopper! The exceptional dining chairs are covered in just the right shade of red, which provides the perfect counterpoint."

**KELLY BEHUN**

"In designing this Moroccan-inspired porch, we wanted to incorporate a healthy dose of saffron, my client's favorite color. In the process, we found these jolts of vivid pink to be a nice counterbalance. Bold and saturated, together they hold their own next to the dazzling turquoise waters and lush green palm trees beyond."

**JAY JEFFERS**

"We designed this New York City apartment with an edited eye, confining the color to red in this lacquered dining room. We carried the red through to the ceiling with a red and gold–patterned wallpaper while keeping the furniture more neutral. We finished with a red-accented rug to tie the whole room together. Repeating red in nuanced ways unifies the room and sets the tone for lively dinner conversation."

**SUMMER THORNTON**

"This room is a color statement if there ever was one. The client wanted a happy living room without too much formality. We took the original boiserie and, inspired by the blue city of Jodhpur, India, swathed the entire room in this vivid blue! We then kept the fun going by layering in two ruby-colored sofas the color of Dorothy's slippers and a few dashes of yellow in the pillows and flowers."

LOUIS VUITTON

MARTYN LAWRENCE BULLARD

"Pink is always one of the most flattering colors to use in a room. The hue makes all who are surrounded by it look healthy and attractive. For maximum effect, I chose to lacquer the ceiling of this bedroom in desert rose and paint the moldings and paneling in the cabinetry the same tone, creating a magical ambience that feels both exotic and inviting."

D'AQUINO MONACO

"In renovating this historic Tuxedo Park, New York, residence for a young family, we adopted a joyful and irreverent approach. By creating a modern 'skin' with a subtle variation of twenty vertical stripes of color that overlay the original architectural detailing from base to crown, a new life has been gifted to this room while retaining its historic stature."

KEVIN ISBELL

"Being part of a larger room overlooking Central Park, this dining area needed a personality of its own. The cool powder-blue Venetian plaster is the perfect foil for the warm tones of the gold satin–upholstered walls in the adjacent living area. The grasshopper-green upholstery and pillows provide the perfect counterpoint—a nod to the verdant trees just outside the windows in spring."

Jeffrey Bilhuber defining LUXURY
VOGUE LIVING COUNTRY CITY COAST

**BROCKSCHMIDT & COLEMAN**

Previous spread: "We selected the warm pumpkin color of this room, which opens off the entrance hall of the house, to give an intimate feel to the space and provide a rich backdrop to the owner's artwork and collections. The luminous paint finish comes from several layers of varnish on top of a standard painted base coat, which is a technique we admired at the Brush-Everard House in Williamsburg, Virginia."

Left: "When this client told us that the one wish for her new home was a plush pink chesterfield sofa, we envisioned tall pink curtains with embroidered valances at the French doors and upholstery in cream with red, fuchsia, and purple accents to provide a sumptuous, feminine Parisian atmosphere that would complement the rich boiserie walls. The pale blues in the painting and deeper blue accents in the antique carpet accentuate the airy character and recall the sky outside the New York penthouse apartment."

**AMANDA NISBET**

"This client took a big leap of faith and trusted me when I proposed a blue, green, pink, orange, yellow, and purple room. The result is gratifying, glorious, and an alchemical color magic."

1008 PIECE PUZZLE
JOHN BARMAN INTERIOR DESIGN
DIANA VREELAND THE MODERN WOMAN
JAY JEFFERS COLLECTED COOL
HOUSES
YORK

**PHILIP GORRIVAN**

"There is nothing bolder—or more satisfying—than making the decision to paint a room a singular color, including the walls, ceiling, and trim. In this case, layers of lacquer in shades of Granny Smith–apple green in this New York City entry create a pleasing and visually delicious result! The sculptural table completes the maximalist feeling we were going for."

**DRAKE / ANDERSON**

"For big impact, we love to use a single color throughout a room. Varying the textures creates depth and interest: in this room, the walls are upholstered in a contemporary damask with subtle shimmer; the sofa wears plush velvet; and brass, gilt, and bronze tables, accessories, and a mirror amplify the effect."

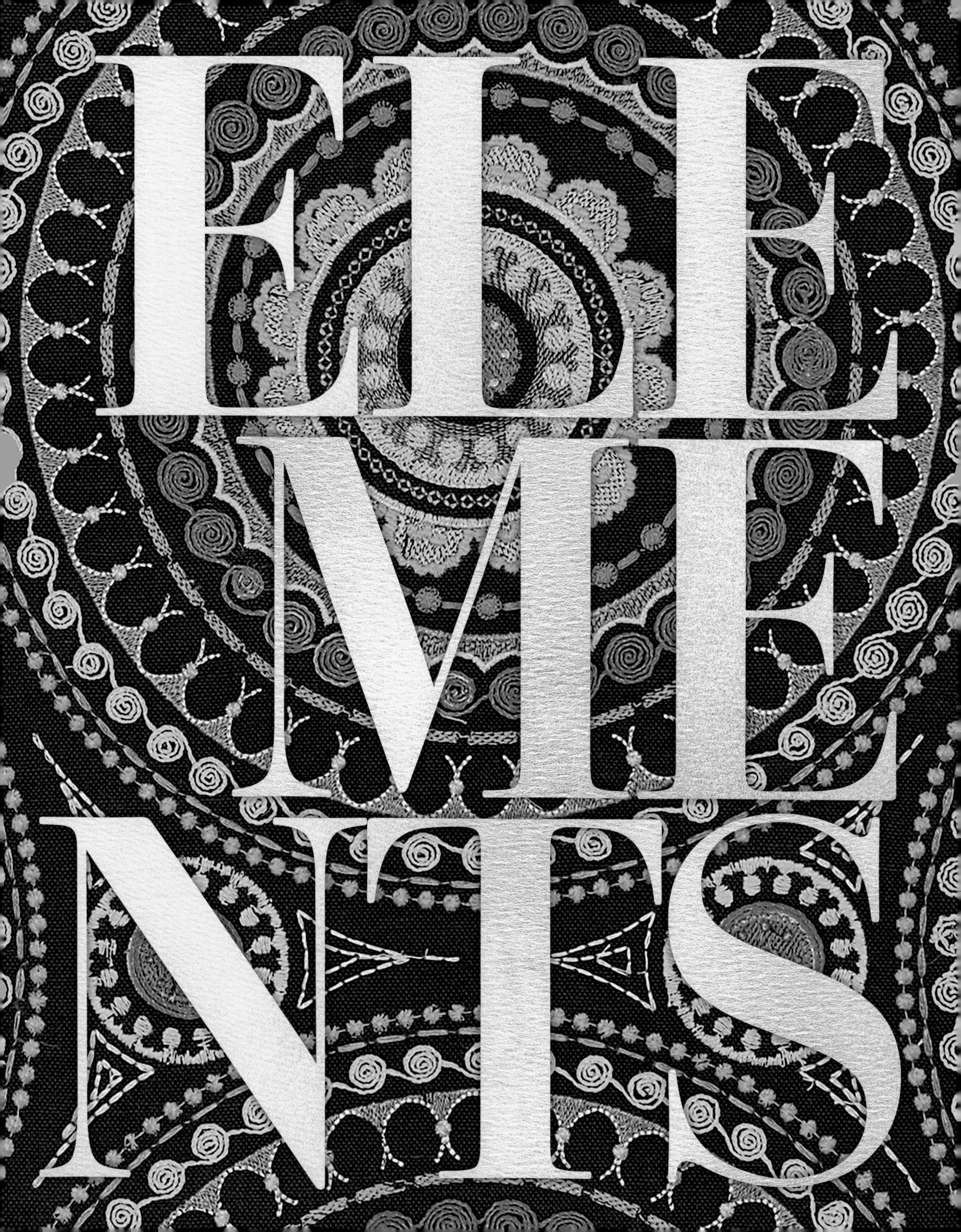
ELE
ME
NTS

THERE ARE TIMES WHEN A MAXIMALIST INTERIOR IS DEFINED by a singular element, challenging the typical maximalist convention of a densely populated room that combines a myriad of finishes and furnishings. In these unique spaces, paradoxically speaking, less can be maximalist too. On the other hand, there are rooms where a single design element is used multiple times—either densely populated in one area or scattered throughout—adding visual interest and maximalist flair. However a potent element is utilized, it can carry a space, becoming a focal point that punctuates a room in a superlative way.

As a rule of thumb, using an element or elements in a maximalist manner can be successfully achieved in three primary ways: through the manipulation of scale; through the singularity of an element; and, in the case of collections, through repetition.

On the subject of scale, I'm reminded of what legendary designer Juan Montoya wrote on the subject in my book *Interior Design Master Class*: "Create a focal point from the best pieces you can muster. Dare to be imposing. Even a small room may take on majesty if one orchestrates, sparingly, significant pieces within it: large in size, superb in style, and high in quality."

Several rooms in this chapter exemplify the ideas Montoya puts forth. One in particular is the wood-paneled entryway of a stately Tudor-style home, spare and rather austere, with an immense sculptural foot by the Italian artist Gaetano Pesce centered on an unadorned floor. Another features a piece of functional sculpture in the form of a monumental door—commissioned by the designers—set off by uniquely faceted walls. In both cases, exaggerated scale telegraphs an arresting more-is-more feeling. But when going for grand gestures, there is one caveat: dynamic pieces benefit from negative space around them, so that they can be fully appreciated.

With regard to singularity, an element in a room might stand out for its rarity or the way it's been positioned in relation to other elements, allowing it to take center stage. An illustration you'll find in this chapter is an antique mirrored tester bed positioned on a grand-scaled stenciled floor and surrounded by serene pink walls.

Perhaps the idea most easily employed in maximalist interior design is the repetition of an element. Designers return again and again to this idea as a way to turn up the volume in a room. One fine example in this chapter is the ceiling of an elegant Dallas living room, which is covered in crisp, white-painted decorative plaster blocks. And there are several glorious rooms with a collection of artworks hung gallery-style that collectively command attention.

Whatever the approach, one thing is paramount: choosing the elements of a maximalist space should be an enjoyable process. Pick elements that you respond to emotionally, elements that you will be happy to live with. Joy is a precious commodity, so by all means have it in abundance at home.

58

**REDD KAIHOI**

"The entire ceiling was glass in this Los Angeles sunroom, which proved to be too much sun at midday. So we added a creative design element—a sheer retractable awning—which cut the light and made you want to be in the room throughout the day."

**D'AQUINO MONACO**

"A custom pair of interlocking cast-resin doors were designed as a single sculptural element in this conception of contemporary urban luxury living. They elegantly conceal the sitting area that's part of the primary suite in this apartment."

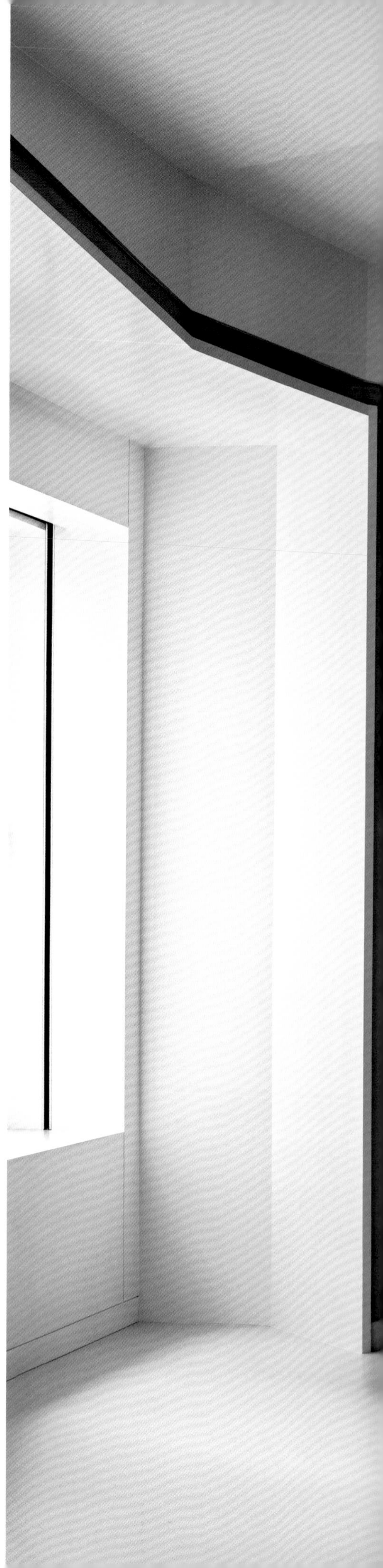

### COMMUNE DESIGN

"This mural was commissioned from Louis Eisner, a young painter based in New York. He took the limited color range from the incredible Malibu coast just outside and created an abstraction of the coastal view. Not only did the painting bring all the colors and elements in the room together, it also quite literally expanded the view as intended. Much like the coast itself, the colors dramatically change with the light throughout the day."

### BUNNY WILLIAMS

Opposite: "No matter the style of your home, it's the personal possessions that make your rooms unique and express your personality. The base of this room is quite simple, but the textiles, art, and objects I've collected over time give it character. Intimacy in an interior comes when there is a blend. Not everything needs to match."

Overleaf: "I've changed certain elements of my bedroom as I've moved from one apartment to the next, but this mirrored bed—a 1940s piece by Parisian designer Serge Roche—always stays. It feels like a piece of jewelry. I love the way every piece is tapered or beveled, and the height makes the room feel taller. The headboard is Indian silk that I had embroidered based on an antique textile I found, and the painted floor keeps the room feeling open and light."

MICHAEL CONNELLY THE LATE SHOW
The Latecomers HELEN KLEIN ROSS
The Rise and Fall of
ANCIENT EGYPT
TOBY WILKINSON

DONNA LEON
THE HUNTRESS
COLIN DEXTER

BLOWOUT

ELKINS

ALEXANDER DOHERTY

"In my living room, I have a large collection of twentieth-century paintings that I am constantly adding to. There is no real method behind the buying, but I do find I'm very much drawn to pieces that are geometric and quite colorful. I love surrounding myself with artwork, so I am constantly rehanging in order to accommodate new purchases. I never take into consideration a room's furnishings when it comes to artwork. I think art should be able to stand alone."

CAREY McGUIRE WARMAN

Left: "I love that great art creates emotion and conversation. And a giant foot by Italian sculptor Gaetano Pesce, used here as the focal point of this entry, just makes you smile. It sets the tone for curiosity in the home as soon as you walk in."

Overleaf: "Keeping the walls, ornate ceiling, floors, and even the wall sculpture pure white establishes a beautifully neutral, textural backdrop that allows the table, chairs, and light fixture to feel more like the sculpture of the room. It's a gallery-style approach even though it's a fully functional dining room."

Van Cleef & Arpels

**NICK OLSEN**

"This room is rather long and narrow with awkward corners, so my clients had no idea how to arrange it and used it for storage. I imagined it as a den, designing this modern sectional sofa to fit in one niche and finding a perfectly scaled desk to sit adjacent to it. The lacquered walls and sofa velvet match exactly, and the carpet is a soft solid-colored cowhide. This combination allows the boldly printed Roman shade and dramatic oil painting to become focal points in the room."

**DENISE McGAHA**

"The drama of a maximalist ceiling can't be overstated, but remember to balance it with the other elements in the room. We designed this room with neutrals and accented it with antiques and important artwork to offset the patterned plaster ceiling, which we painted white. The abundant natural light allows the play of shadow to constantly change, which is quite special."

**AMANDA LANTZ**

"When implementing a maximalist approach to a space, it's important to consider geometry and the rhythm of the room while grounding the movement with some repetition of shapes and styles. Here, art becomes the focal element of the design with the use of vintage pieces, newly framed works, and a large commissioned painting by my father, Barry Lantz."

INSIDE HOLLYWOOD
LIFE MEETS ART
HOUSES IN MY HEART
A ROOM of ONE'S
IN THE PINK
THE CROWN JEWELS

ART LIFE

**BRADFORD SHELLHAMMER**

"The staircase is the first thing you see when you walk into this house in upstate New York. To the left is a black-and-white great room; to the right, the library and music rooms in red and blue. To finish the primary-color trifecta, I chose high-gloss yellow paint. I wanted it to look like lemon candy melting down the steps, creating a unique design element to greet guests."

**KATIE CURTIS**

Overleaf, left: "The client is from South America at the foot of the Andes mountains, so this wallcovering with the abstract mountain pattern was chosen initially as a reference to their heritage. We all loved the original colorway the hand-painted paper came in, and that became the basis of the color story for the room."

Overleaf, right: "The chandelier was chosen for its mountain-like facets. The room features a great mix of old and new, raw and refined, and this piece gives the space an edgier feel in contrast to its soft linens and velvets."

I'm only arrogant because I'm afraid you'll find out I'm ordinary.
STAY
DON'T
VORRY
YOU
WON'
SAVE T
WORL

ITALY
Lalanne

**DRAKE / ANDERSON**

Previous spread: "Sculptural elements energize a room with their unique presence, and here we used sinuous and curvaceous forms as a contrast to the rectilinear background. A swooping, extruded traditional chair form is functional art, the tower of silvered orbs talks with the circular motif screen across the space, and a sweeping wave drop ceiling covered in silver leaf defines the dining area while helping us tame some unruly beams."

Overleaf: "In a large, square great room, a range of colors and silhouettes come together to create a personality-packed environment. Sensuously curved shapes covered in vibrant fabrics command special attention and create delightful variation from the geometric."

**STEVEN GAMBREL**

"Two biomorphic ottomans, clad in pumpkin-orange leather and piped in blue, introduce organic shapes in this Greenwich Village family room. As design elements, they are both functional and playful, and as they age, they'll gather a wonderful patina. The Roman shades were tailored from a Missoni chevron-patterned fabric, which informs the room's color scheme. The pearl-toned lacquered ceiling magnifies the midday sun, while the Sputnik chandeliers come alive at night, bouncing an amber glow."

BAUHAUS
TOM FORD
MANDELA
PALAZZI OF SICILY

ROBERT POLIDORI HAVANA

MARKET VALUE
GRAFT
STIMATED VALUE
ROME PAYS OFF
SALT

AMERICAN

### MARTYN LAWRENCE BULLARD

"In the primary bedroom of my Palm Springs home, I used an expansive screen covered in my Raleigh Stripe fabric to anchor the room for maximum impact. The bold terrazzo floor and artwork play a part in the dramatic setting, but the screen's commanding presence frames the bed and nightstands while simultaneously claiming its star power in the space."



### GIDEON MENDELSON

"The goal was to create a dramatic and glamorous dining room for these clients in the West Village neighborhood of New York City. We combined contemporary and midcentury-inspired elements for an eclectic look. Brass, wood, marble, and wallpaper ensure that no surface is left unadorned. The result is a maximalist interior, the perfect setting to spark compelling dinner conversation."

### KEN FULK

Overleaf, left: "The powder room is anchored by a monumental sink carved from a single slab of marble by the very talented Jim Gray. This house is a study in old-world techniques, and this powder room is a miniature shrine to custom craftsmanship with its stained-glass windows and sunbeam chandelier."

Overleaf, right: "Zebra print is remarkable in its ability to be both timeless and contemporary—similar to the mix of portraiture decorating the entry walls. Here the multitude of figures, patterns, materials, and colors feels cohesive under the rich red canopy of the lacquered ceiling."

# PATTERN

NINGHAM: ON THE STREET
OGRAPHIC UNIVERSE

IN MY FORMER CAREER AS A TEXTILE DESIGNER, PATTERN was an omnipresent concern. Creating a design element and then engineering it to echo across the width and length of fabric was challenging yet very enjoyable work. And while stripes have always been a personal fascination, there's a vast, ever-expanding trove of patterns for designers to utilize in maximalist rooms.

The patterns in use today have their origins in many cultures, with motifs originating from East to West. There are time-honored Persian paisleys, both traditional and contemporary interpretations; adaptations of ancient Roman herringbones in every color of the rainbow; ginghams, which are thought to be of Malaysian origin, from the Malay word *genggang*; tree-of-life designs born from Indian bedcovers and tent panels called palampores; and bountiful florals traced back to China and subsequently reinvented by Europeans.

As dizzying as the breadth of patterns that exist is, there is an equally vast number of ways in which interior designers can deploy them. A grand-scaled William Morris design from the mid-nineteenth-century founder of the Arts and Crafts movement might be papered around the perimeter of a library, creating a kinetic rhythm. An awning stripe fashioned into tasteful curtains hung from lacquered white rods can serve to impose order on the landscape just outside the window. And speaking of outside, an English floral chintz, covering a range of upholstery silhouettes, transports the visitor to the gardens of a historic Essex manor house in the languishing days of a British summer.

Then there's the artful juxtaposition of patterns, giving maximalist designers an opportunity to mix and match to create a range of effects. A decadent salon sheathed in an electrifying mix can feel like a 1990s Christian Lacroix haute couture runway show, providing the backdrop for invigorating conversation. Alternately, a demure bedroom with patterns that reveal a graceful mix of motifs encourages a sense of serenity just before slumber. There's always something that creates a connection—either overtly or in a nuanced way.

Repetition of color is one tried-and-true option for mixing patterns in successful maximalist rooms. For example, a chevron-patterned rug woven in brown and white would pair perfectly with a Moorish-motif wallpaper similarly inflected with brown and accented by powder blue and silver. Repeating motifs works just as well: a delicate Indian lotus print on a tablecloth trimmed with a deep bullion fringe would mix perfectly with a blossoming peony fabric on a collection of throw pillows. The mix could be further unified by a rose-covered Aubusson underfoot, resulting in a verdant botanical flair.

Utilizing geographical references is also an excellent way to link patterns. Think wallpaper populated with chinoiserie pagodas set against a bamboo trellis upholstered on a pair of club chairs, then paired with a stylized chrysanthemum-covered folding screen. To take this idea a step further, a designer might choose a variety of locales by combining a Francophile toile, a Portuguese azulejo, and a Florentine vine, tracing a path around Europe.

With the vast knowledge the designers in this book possess on the history of the decorative arts—coupled with their curiosity and intuition—it's no surprise that the rooms in this chapter brim with the creative use of pattern. As they would likely all agree, using patterns successfully comes down to what appeals to us personally. To quote the legendary decorator Billy Baldwin, "Be faithful to your own taste, because nothing you really like is ever out of style."

**SUMMER THORNTON**

Previous spread: “I’m of the mind that the more pattern, the better. The more you layer it, the cozier a room gets. I especially love this trick for an architecturally awkward room. It distracts the eye and turns a bland space into one that people are drawn to. Here we stuck to a consistent palette of deep indigo blues for maximum impact.”

Right: “In this dining room, we used pattern to add a structural element to the space; the wallpaper gives the illusion of architectural sophistication while adding a bit of grandeur. I love the busyness of the paper mixed with the myriad of additional stripes, florals, and animal prints to create the ultimate maximalist dream tablescape.”

Overleaf: “This cozy little TV den is made memorable by all-over tiny pattern matching. Arbre de Matisse is an artful pattern inspired by the painter’s work. I was inspired by that oh-so-famous image of Billy Baldwin’s own apartment with that fabulous sofa and chair in this iconic print. We decided to take it up a notch and match it to the walls to create a cocoon-like effect. We layered in Matisse-inspired pops of color on top of all the rich brown.”

HARRY HEISSMANN

Right: "For this exuberantly patterned bedroom, I adopted a client-centric approach. They asked me to create a tropical garden in a Florida high-rise with views of the Intracoastal Waterway, Palm Beach island, and the Atlantic Ocean. To complete the task, I chose Pierre Frey's Bonsai. Note how the scale of the pattern is slightly different on the fabric and wallpaper, which serendipitously adds a sense of dimensionality."

Overleaf: "We decided on a black-and-white theme for this guest bedroom, which we accented with a deep watermelon shade. The wallpaper is from Schumacher; it sets an exotic Moroccan tone, which we juxtaposed against a floral bed covering. The coordinating wallpaper borders at the ceiling and floor add an architectural element to the space."

### GARROW KEDIGIAN

"I wanted this dining room to exude playfulness, so I used the dining chairs to diffuse the formality of the paneled walls around the room's perimeter. The chevron-patterned material we selected conjures that whimsical feeling we were looking for; the waves help the chairs 'dance' around the table, while the color subtly and elegantly draws attention to the center of the room."

### REDD KAIHOI

Opposite: "The beauty of Manhattan apartment living is stepping through a front door into a completely new world. This entrance hall is the fantasy child of a Medici and M.C. Escher. Covering the foyer and main artery, the enveloping pattern disguises the practical elements of living behind multiple hidden doors, like a laundry room and closets for coats, linens, and guests."

Overleaf: "While this log cabin is located in the Adirondack Mountains, the directive was to make it more like Gstaad. We love the play of pattern against pattern and the contrast of rustic and high style. It is always the tension between disparate elements that makes a room exciting."

### MARKHAM ROBERTS

Previous spread, left: "In the dining room of the late nineteenth-century sea captain's cottage overlooking Puget Sound that I share with my partner, James Sansum, I upholstered the walls with a Décors Barbares print designed by my longtime friend Nathalie Farman-Farma that I custom colored to work in the room. The similarly colored yet differently scaled pattern of the Bessarabian rug is effective in tying the two patterns together without being repetitive."

Previous spread, right: "The living room of this waterfront house, which overlooks a bird sanctuary on Nantucket Bay, carries a riot of patterns from all different periods and geographic and cultural origins, symbolizing the great American melting pot in an old-fashioned Yankee way, set against austere white-painted wood planking."

Overleaf: "By using blues of different values and slightly varying hues in the bedroom of this house on Nantucket, the color palette—though limited to blue and white—becomes more visually interesting and less 'matchy.' Adding the pink contrast on the antique American quilt helps to relax any feeling of rigidity."

### MARTYN LAWRENCE BULLARD

"In this Palm Springs guest room, maximal drama and a sense of place are captured with the use of pattern on pattern. The scene is set with Schumacher's Zebra Palm wallpaper and amped up by a Rug Company chevron dhurrie on a harlequin terrazzo floor. A bed throw by Kelly Wearstler plays against the pillow fabrics, reinforcing my theory that when it comes to patterns, never be afraid to layer—and then layer again!"

PRIVATE

TOULOUSE-LAUTREC
FRENCH RIVIERA IN THE 1920s
LIFE MEETS ART
JANSEN

MOULIN ROUGE
MISTINGUETT
Hector Guimard

**CREATIVE TONIC**

"Inspired by the opulent interiors of the belle époque era with a nod to Maison Jansen, I called on brilliant colors, richly layered textiles, and dressmaker details for this media room, all imbued with a modern twist. This combination is bold and dramatic, yet nuanced and sensual. It is exactly what it would feel like to step inside a genie bottle for movie night!"

**CHRISTINA JAUREZ**

"A circular painting by Takashi Murakami sets a playful tone for my bedroom, which I chose to unify with recurring shades of lavender and purple. Choosing one color throughout creates cohesion, even with a mix of patterns. The green glassware from The End of History in the West Village adds an important counterpoint—like the leaves on a lilac branch in spring."

**NICK OLSEN**

"Mixing patterns is all about scale, and in this bedroom each one is given ample relief. A playful ribbon appliqué on the curtain panels coordinates with a fine embroidered stripe on the settee. Vintage paisley scatter rugs cover the floor and complement a suzani bedcover and the block-print on the walls. The patterns don't compete with one another since each has a different scale and color intensity."

VERANDA
CROSS PURPOSE

SNOW FALLING
JANELLE BROWN
SHOBHA RAO
THE POWER TO COMPETE
THE COUPLE NEXT DOOR
GRIFFITH

**KATIE CURTIS**

Previous spread: "The varying scales of the patterns in this expansive room create the story. There is a hierarchy and order to the selections: the medium-scale pattern on the upholstered chairs is smaller than the wallpaper, but large enough to work with the sofa and loveseat. The scale of patterns on the throw pillows adds to the mix.The vintage tribal rug grounds the room perfectly and brings everything together."

Overleaf: "This client loves purple, and purple is difficult to get right. It can easily skew juvenile or sweet, neither of which we were looking for. The room is expansive with high ceilings, so we needed a pattern that would humanize the scale. We kept the palette monochromatic, letting the wallpaper be the star of the show: it's pretty but not too girly, and there is an edginess about it that pairs well with the nickel elements in the four-poster bed. The velvet coverlet and inlay chests on either side of the bed add textural interest."

**JAY JEFFERS**

"The primary bedroom of this California home leans into a few varying but complementary patterns: the rug, the pillows, and the room's focal point—a custom hide wall by Kyle Bunting. The result is a room that's modern, eclectic, and comfortable, while embodying the bright personality of its owner."

Peter Lindbergh
A Different Vision on Fashion Photography
TASCHEN

### MADCAP COTTAGE

"Pattern, pattern, and more patterns take center stage in this Brooklyn guest bedroom. It's a floral fantasy come to life, bolstered with punches of bold color such as coral, pink, and yellow. Brown wood furnishings help to ground the pattern explosion. And, yes, you can layer artwork upon a busy wallpaper. Play with scale to make the mix magical: think smaller prints paired with larger-scale options to keep the eye engaged."

### MARK D. SIKES

Overleaf, left: "I chose the mirror above the mantel as a complement to the wallpaper; the shape echoes the patterns and motifs as your eye travels around the room. The solid blue upholstery on the loveseat and ivory curtains balance out the intricate detail throughout. The table you see is not a desk, but a library table that divides the seating areas. The dark antiques are Italian and very rare; their darker tones are the perfect contrast to the light blues in the room."

Overleaf, right: "The wallpaper was custom designed with Iksel and serves as the foundation of the room. I complemented its intricate pattern with a geometric dhurrie; the rug also tones down the room and makes it feel more casual. On the walls, the porcelain plates and vases on brackets add dimension. We wanted it to feel like the pattern had a three-dimensional effect."

ROMA

JOHN RAWLINGS 30 Years in Vogue
CY TWOMBLY DRAWINGS
PALMS

# LAYERING

DESIGNERS AT HOME
Private Gardens of Connecticut
HAIR
Suas gu Deas
MANNAHATTA
TRADITIONAL HOME
TADAO ANDO

AS THE TITLE OF THIS BOOK SUGGESTS, "MORE IS MORE" is the ethos of maximalism, and layering is the best implement in a designer's toolbox to achieve maximalist flair. Color, finishes, materials, furnishings, and organic elements create rooms that have a larger maximalist impact than the sum of their parts. Think of it like a musical composition: each instrumental layer adds to the richness of a piece. When violins, cellos, clarinets, drums, flutes, oboes, saxophones, and French horns combine, they build toward an exhilarating crescendo as exciting as the rooms in this chapter.

But there is one important clarification: not every layered room can be considered maximalist. For example, rooms conceived around neutral color schemes with nuanced textures and quiet, luxurious furnishings may be rich in supremely sophisticated layers and yet not over the top in any way.

While not every layered room is maximalist, nearly every maximalist room is layered. In fact, the more richly layered a space, the more maximalist it becomes. The rooms in this book explode with such enthusiasm, exuberantly telegraphing the creativity of the designers behind each space.

Collected interiors reveal themselves in stages and over time as the eye establishes relationships between parts of an interior. These include the finishes in a room, like wallpaper, paint, wood, stone, textiles, and passementerie.

Then textures begin to appear as more complex layers reveal themselves: the coarse grain of rough-hewn walnut used in a shiplap wall treatment, the sheen of the highly polished marble top on a brass-framed coffee table, the chunky comfort of lush chenille upholstered onto a headboard.

As the eye travels around a room, we perceive elements in slightly larger groups: the massed decorative pillows positioned on upholstered pieces astride patterned rugs, or lacquered walls punctuated by luxurious window treatments and a handsome, geometric hand-stenciled floor.

Plants add another layer—either singularly, like the large-scale rich green leaves of a fiddlehead fig tree, or in concert with one another, like a pair of Boston ferns on pedestals near a spiky Christmas cactus in full riotous bloom.

Collections play a key role in maximizing rooms. A dozen tall Murano glass vases in differing hues would command attention on a center hall table, but their impact is enhanced even more by an assortment of Moroccan marquetry boxes interspersed with antique candlesticks.

Books are a valuable component of any layered room; they imbue a space with a certain sense of knowledge while revealing the interests of the home's inhabitants. When grouped with other personal mementos, such as generations of family snapshots in silver picture frames or seashells gathered from an annual sojourn to a much-loved beach, a family's history is revealed on the shelves.

Ask any of the designers represented in these pages, and they'll surely tell you that when a maximalist room is layered correctly, it feels effortless—despite the skill it took to create—with each finish, material, furnishing, and object in equilibrium. It's the secret sauce of decorating. Like the pieces of an elaborate jigsaw puzzle, a maximalist room comes into focus when every piece, every loop and socket, is connected and in its place.

**ROBERT PASSAL**

"I build my interiors so that they appear as an evolution—homes that have grown and changed with their owners. Layers of fabrics, rugs, art, collections, books, worldly finds, and accessories tell a story about the life, history, and interests of those who inhabit the space."

**VIRGINIA TUPKER**

"I love color and mixing clashing prints. Start slowly with a simple solid base and build from there. Lauren Santo Domingo's barn is a great example. Here, found vintage textiles add warmth and character to the space and inspired the final palette and direction for the room."

de Kooning
POSTWAR
TONY JUDT
TEAM OF RIVALS
THE THORN BIRDS
david sedaris
PEPYS
Princesses
LOUIS XIV
GALILEO'S DAUGHTER
ROOM 606

MILES REDD THE BIG BOOK OF CHIC
ASHLEY HICKS

**PAMELA BLACK & DON LOVE**

"We were fortunate in the fact that this room, being the heart of the home, was generous in size so we could propose numerous seating areas. The fabrics and trims really tell the story here, which further dictated the wall color, lighting, floor covering, and art. These building blocks are reflected throughout the room, from layering the accent rugs atop the woven sisal to the specific shade of silk that lined a lampshade—nothing was left unappointed! For us, it's all about the emotional response to the finished space. It's the sum of all parts, both physically and mentally."

**D'AQUINO MONACO**

"We adopted a joyful and irreverent approach to this elegant summer residence built in 1911. Framed art by the family's children is hung in the gothic paneled library, thereby infusing a dark room with fun and brightness. The unexpected use of color and pattern adds whimsy to the otherwise traditional space. In doing so, a new life was brought to this home while retaining its historical significance."

**PIERCE & WARD**

"We never want a room to feel overly 'designed,' and something that can help with that is to really mix it up. Buy things you love even if you don't think they have a spot, because there is always a spot! If objects and finishes in a room appeal to you individually, then they are sure to harmonize when mixed together."

HOLLYWOOD BABYLON
ALEXANDER McQUEEN: SAVAGE BEAUTY

**ELIZABETH LAWRENCE** ▶

"The wallcovering, which we had digitally printed, was inspired by the intricate zellige tilework found in Morocco. The elephant table and mix of textiles on the sectional also reinforce this sense of travel, but the color palette, which is grounded in a soft blue, was taken from the view of the ocean outside the windows and lends a sense of place."

**ANDREW BROWN** ▼

"When designing a room, I frequently incorporate a stenciled floor into the mix to add dimension to a space. I prefer a large-scale pattern to keep the floor from becoming too 'busy' and work smaller complementary patterns into the furnishings. I also pull colors from the stenciled floor and spread them throughout the room with throw pillows and upholstered pieces to tie everything together and achieve balance."

RAJASTHAN

A WANDERING EYE
NEW YORK SPLENDOR
Wendy Moonan

AMERICAN FASHION

MR. KEN·FULK'S·MAGICAL·WOR

CREATIVE TONIC

"This is what I call high-contrast neutral! While I'm generally drawn to vibrant bursts of color, layering luscious textures in a moody, monochromatic palette channels an ambience of subtle excess just as beautifully. Rather than relying on color to generate maximalism, I created a feast for the eyes by mixing luscious textures like worn leather, shaved velvet, and metallic grass cloth with fun geometric forms, unusual copper tubing, and collected vintage and contemporary art finds and photography."

ASHLEY WHITTAKER

Opposite: "In this Greenwich, Connecticut, dining room, we combined different periods, finishes, materials, and scales. The chalky-white Louis XVI–style chairs contrast with the dark Cuban mahogany table, while the rustic floors and lacquered walls are a counterpoint to one another. Mixing old with new and light with dark adds dimension to any space. Contrast automatically creates layered style."

Overleaf: "Scenic wallpaper can serve as a starting point: sometimes it's the color of the tail feather of a bird from which you pull the Prussian blue for the sofa fabric or lamp. That same blue might be the color on lacquered walls in a room beyond, which helps to draw a visual connection. It is often color that marries rooms together to establish the decorative thread of a house."

THE WORLD IN VOGUE

HICKS

I AM A CAMERA

## REATH DESIGN

"We love when our clients come to the table with pieces they have collected through the years. This particular client was downsizing, so we got to pull a collection of our favorite pieces from her larger house to combine them in a new way in this sitting room. The hand-printed Marthe Armitage wallpaper added a patina; it feels like it has been there for years."

## COMMUNE DESIGN

"This California dining room is a repository of layered elements that combine beautifully. The posters are original Cuban propaganda posters from the 1960s; their colors and graphics set the tone, with everything else falling into place around them. The table and chairs were made by furniture collector and designer Michael Boyd. The cabinet is a Paul McCobb piece, and the pendant is from Commune's collection for Remains Lighting. The curtains were commissioned from textile artist Adam Pogue and look like stained glass."

## BROCKSCHMIDT & COLEMAN

"In my own New York loft apartment, minimalism was not an option due to the square footage and my penchant for collecting, so the architecture was designed especially for layering books, artwork, and objects collected while traveling. Not only walls and flat surfaces are embellished with treasures, but also bookcases and door surrounds. Even the staircase doubles as a bookcase, with a collection of niches." —Bill Brockschmidt

FESTIVAL DE LA CANCION
FESTIVAL OF POPULAR
FESTIVAL DE LA CHANSON

Italian
On Distant Shores
CASA GUASTAMALTICA
VENICE

IN THE PINK
CHICAGO APARTMENTS
Irish houses & castles
OPERA
THOMAS JEFFERSON
Sir William Chambers
Peerless Images
Adoration and Glory
THE WAY WE LIVE
TEXAS

**PHILIP MITCHELL**

"To create a warm and welcoming space, layer texture and depth in everything from fabrics and rugs to furnishings and artwork. Don't be afraid of mixing patterns and colors; think of textiles as works of art that can add personality and style to a room."

**MATTHEW MONROE BEES**

"Mixing antiques from different periods and cultures is an excellent way to add layers to a room, and a contemporary Lucite table adds just the right counterpoint. Don't be afraid of bright colors—they add a layer of freshness while modernizing heirloom silhouettes. The textured wallpaper from Thibaut and the zebra-hide rug, casually placed over whitewashed heart-pine floors, add texture to the space."

**PATRICK MELE**

"My client wanted a space to dive right into—an inviting, luxurious, plush, and richly textured room for her family's laid-back life. To accomplish this, I layered an eighteenth-century matte damask wallpaper, reflective lacquer, ruby-colored crystal, brass, opaline, leopard print, antique ikats, and florals from vintage scarves with antiques collected over time. This room and its components feel alive, like a worldly banquet for the senses with the utmost bohemian flair."

**KEN FULK**

"This study is anchored by a pair of engraved art nouveau club chairs, a chesterfield sofa, and a painting by James Weeks, but the magic is in the more subtle mix—the architectural details in the tracery ceiling and paneling complement the collection of furniture, accessories, and books."

**REDD KAIHOI**

"This room is a collection of objects built around tobacco-brown velvet and the eau-de-Nil wallcovering, which are colors that appear in the rug on the floor. We like to establish the floors and walls and then build from there. The resulting room has seemingly infinite layers that reveal themselves over time."

Leonardo da Vinci
Allure Diana Vreeland
Complete Works

BAUHAUS
WITH THE BEATLES
CAROLINA HERRERA

SAMPLE BOOK
MODERN ARCHITECTURE A-L
BECKMANN & AMERICA
PIANO
PLANT
THE ART OF ROCK
impressionism
HORST

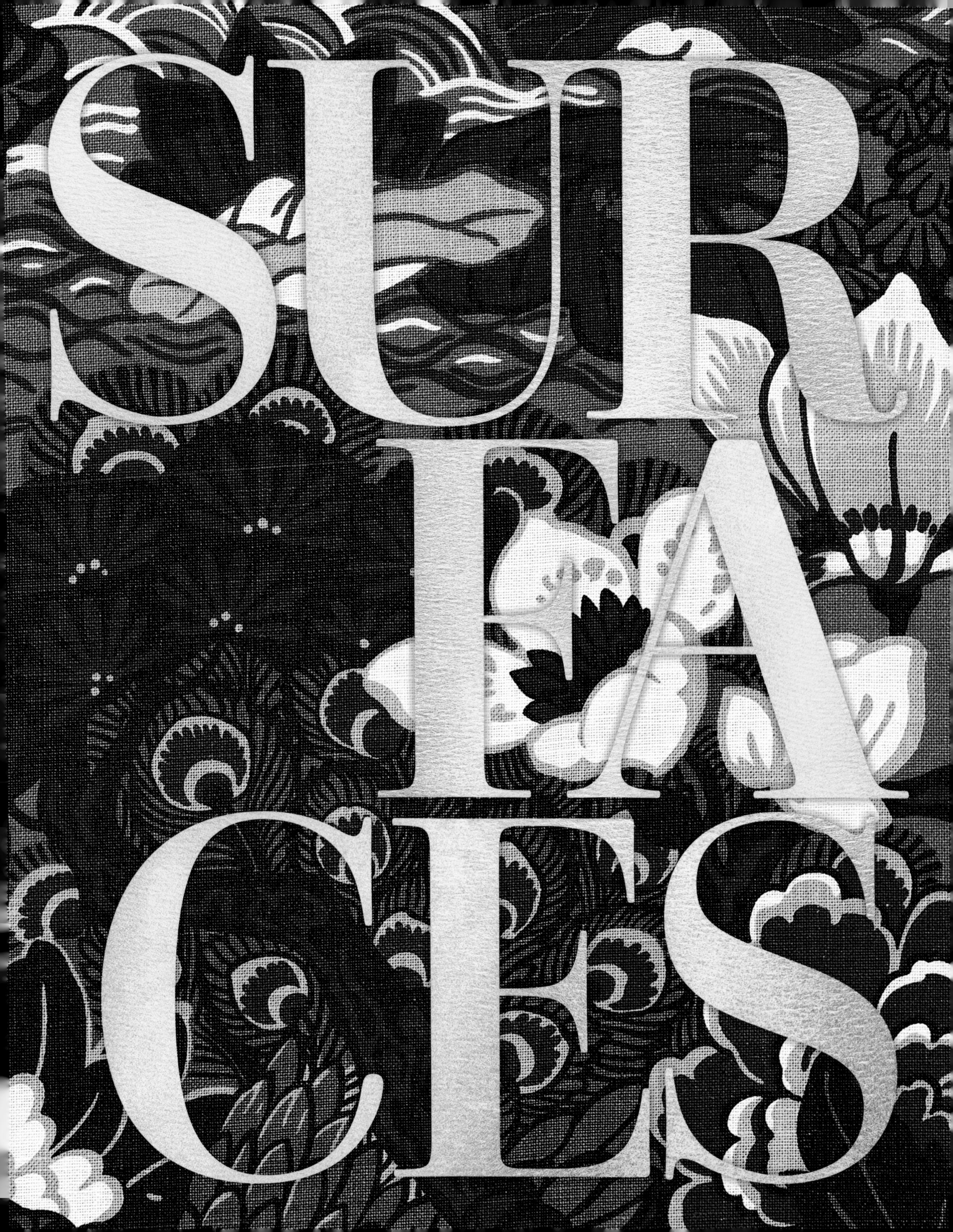
SUR
FA
CES

IN SEARCH OF Rex Whistler
ROMANTIC GARDENS

# SURFACES

NO BOOK ABOUT MAXIMALIST INTERIOR DESIGN WOULD BE complete without mention of Tony Duquette, one of the genre's most celebrated practitioners, who combined fantasy, theatricality, and audacity in equal measure. His aesthetic steeped in global references, Duquette conjured rooms that appear otherworldly, with every surface embellished in wonderfully imaginative ways: Styrofoam fruit crates attached to a ceiling and painted, trompe l'oeil malachite in rich verdant green sheathing the walls, and black-and-white checkerboard floors overlaid haphazardly with gloriously patterned rugs.

Like Duquette, contemporary interior designers know that the majority of rooms are created with a cube or rectangle as their framework. And these rooms have six surfaces: four walls, the floor, and the ceiling. Combined, those six planes create an envelope within which designers can realize endless maximalist ideas.

Because of the number of square feet involved, the four walls of a room provide designers with the biggest way to pack a maximalist punch—both by utilizing standard finishes like wallpaper and paint and by envisioning one-of-a-kind surfaces created by artisans. A good example is walls conceived with bold, graphic patterns or a mix of patterns, or walls that juxtapose a matte finish against lacquer, allowing the light to change as it moves from surface to surface. An adventurous designer might create walls that stand in stark contrast to a room's furnishings—perhaps a stylized floral wallpaper set off by a clean-lined Parsons table. These are just a few ways to decorate vertical planes to enhance a maximalist space. You'll find many more striking and unusual wall treatments in the pages of this chapter.

The floor is the fifth surface in a room, and it has one intrinsic requirement: it must be durable. No matter the material or finish, the floor must withstand the punishment of daily traffic, children, and pets. The good news? Maximalist patterned floors, like a geometric carpet or an intricately tiled mosaic, hide a multitude of sins. In the case of the latter, stone often looks better as it ages; the same could be said for wood floors. Patinated surfaces imbue a room with a sense of history and grace.

Turning to the sixth surface in every room, the ceiling, the legendary twentieth-century decorator Albert Hadley once said, "Ceilings must always be considered. They are the most neglected surface in a room." Contemporary maximalist designers would surely agree with Hadley. High-gloss lacquered or mirrored ceilings reflect light and add drama; wallpapered ceilings draw the eye up and can be everything from restful to kinetic. For the adventurous designer, the sky's the limit—pun intended—when it comes to decorating the ceiling.

Finally, a note of caution: not every surface should be over the top. On the contrary, maximalist rooms benefit when they strike a balance, with some surfaces receding and others taking center stage. A juxtaposition of pattern, color, and texture, in the words of Diana Vreeland, allows the eye to travel.

### MADCAP COTTAGE

"Ceilings are often overlooked, but shouldn't be. In this High Point, North Carolina, home, a faux-painted tented ceiling overhead whisks guests to another land when they step inside what was once a dark, drab foyer. The hand-painted floors and walls bring the magical story line to life. The resulting effect is whimsical, timeless, fresh, and inviting."

### CREATIVE TONIC

Opposite: "The design of this decadent bathroom started with some old-school onyx, Violetta, and green marble tiles. I love using traditional materials in unexpected ways—I am particularly inspired by the stone surfaces of the 1980s and '90s. Notice that the wall pattern is a smaller version of the floor pattern, and a translucent green onyx countertop creates even more fun. Interpreting marble in a fresh, contemporary way lends an inherent sense of drama, and mixing in patterns with the concentric rectangular millwork is what maximalism is all about!"

Overleaf: "Truly a jewel-box moment, this young family's dining room has a bespoke de Gournay wallcovering hand-painted on antiqued-rose metallic paper. For the floral pattern, I selected custom colors that transform throughout the day as natural light bounces off the pale azure-lacquered ceiling. The ceiling creates not only the illusion of a two-story room, but also an ever-changing dappled effect that moves from day to night in the most romantic, colorful, and dreamlike way."

TOM SCHEERER DECORATES
STAIRCASES

The New Formal
CARLOS MOTA

### CULLMAN & KRAVIS

"In our recent Kips Bay Decorator Show House dining room, titled 'Rhapsody in Blue,' we went for all-out maximalist glam. First, we triple-glazed the walls in a midnight blue, with a luminous finish coat. Then we embellished the walls with custom porcelain paillettes by California artisans Dougall Paulson. The paillettes cascade across the mirrored chimney breast and the walls in an irregular and dynamic pattern."

### KEN FULK

Opposite: "This primary bedroom was inspired by the antique cornice with Venetian velvet panels. Combined with the intricate tracery on the barrel-vaulted ceiling and the large Murano glass chandelier, this spacious sleeping area has a regal feeling."

Overleaf: "This circular dining room features a mural by artist and architectural draftsman Wayne David Hand. Designed as a reference to the sprawling national park right outside the window, this foggy scenic mural allows guests around the table to feel like they are meeting in a secret garden hideaway."

KELLEY
KELLEY
KELLEY
KELLEY

188

**BROCKSCHMIDT & COLEMAN**

Previous spread:"While scenic or exuberant wallpaper is often used in entrance halls, dining rooms, or powder rooms, we enveloped the ground floor of this New Orleans carriage house pied-à-terre in an early 1800s-style marble ashlar wallpaper with a Directoire-era border—all by Adelphi Paper Hangings. Simple ticking slipcovers take a back seat to the wallpaper, magnolia paintings, and bold color accents in the painted trim, Aubusson carpet, lamps, and pillows."

Right: "One of our favorite decorative elements is wallpaper, and we especially love those from Adelphi Paper Hangings. Their historic patterns are charming and unusual, the colors can be endlessly customized, the hand-blocked printing gives an artistic quality to the papers, and perhaps most beautiful of all are the deeply colored matte pigments. In a room like this, we think boldly scaled wallpaper enhances the strong architecture and tall ceilings, and the traditional pattern of the paper and the modern elements complement one another."

Overleaf: "This dramatic pink wallpaper with larger-than-life cranes is obviously a showstopper! Not only does its giant scale effectively add a layer of architecture to a smallish room, its boldness and wit transform the space into a truly transporting environment that feels grander than it is."

**RAYMAN BOOZER**

"This bedroom's design embraces a yearning for travel, independence, and light. The grass cloth wallcovering with feathery stripes tells a rich story on its own, but it serves particularly well as a foundation for layers of intricate design. The wallcovering sets the stage for a symphony of contemporary finishes, antique furnishings, found objects, and modern artwork."

**COREY DAMEN JENKINS**

"Tented rooms trace back to Napoleon, yet their timeless appeal has endured to this day. I love fully draping a room with a luxurious textile like shantung or linen; it's splendid for acoustics, and it projects a magnificent royal energy that envelops you."

**ASHLEY WHITTAKER**

"Large-scale wallcoverings make all the difference when creating a cohesive room—not to mention they can hide a multitude of sins if a room isn't perfectly symmetrical. Carrying the wallcovering up and across the ceiling adds instant charm and makes for the coziest bedrooms."

**ROBERT PASSAL**

"The visual appeal of a room is innately and immediately defined upon approaching it by both color and texture. This space was designed to draw guests in visually with the gestural subtlety of enveloping color. The warmth of the wood, slickness of the Duchess satin drapery, clubby feel of the leather, and texture of the rug unfold as the room slowly reveals itself."

**D'AQUINO MONACO**

"We designed the pixelated dining room rug to be viewed both from above while descending into the room and while walking on it, adding a vibrancy to a formal space. In addition, the scale of the room was engaged through the oversize movie-set mural and two-story sculptural stone fireplace."

**BRADFORD SHELLHAMMER**

"I'm obsessed with iconic designs from the 1960s and '70s, and Marimekko's Unikko is a favorite. I have sweaters, socks, towels, and even a tattoo in the print! I chose it as the theme of this guest bedroom, using it on bedding, upholstery, wallpaper, pillows, and throws. The layering of the same print in different colors and scales counterintuitively creates cohesion and calmness."

D
R
A

### NICK OLSEN

"One great joy of my career is collaborating with brilliant artists like Chris Pearson. He took an inspiration photo from a magazine and painted this rustic design freehand on matte black walls, coming up with clever solutions to unify an asymmetrical space while keeping its neoclassical spirit."

### KEVIN ISBELL

"Nothing is more impactful to a room than a bold, graphic wallpaper. In this New York City townhouse, a custom hand-painted Gracie wallpaper is a complete scene-stealer. The coastal wave pattern is an unexpected discovery in a grand parlor in the middle of a major metropolis, making the room all the more special. The pattern gently bounces the eye around the room and wraps the space with movement and energy. While the architecture of the room is exemplary, the wallpaper is undoubtedly the star of the room."

Don Bachardy

**CAREY McGUIRE WARMAN**

“Instead of adding a rug, we painted the floor with a falling-block pattern in surprising colors that will develop the most beautiful patina over time. Using a green from the floor pattern on the walls creates an enveloping feel.”

**STEVEN GAMBREL**

Opposite: “The already generous natural light in this high-style kitchen is enhanced and amplified by all the reflective surfaces I chose for the space: mosaic tile that gently curves across the arched ceiling; cabinetry lacquered in just the right shade of gray; and brass and bronze accents throughout. The patterned floor introduces a geometric element, while the American art deco pendant illuminates the space in the evening. A purple La Cornue range and custom hood anchor one end of the room.”

Overleaf: “In this expansive Greenwich Village game room, the silver-and-gold metallic walls are complemented by floor-to-ceiling arches that I chose to clad in an églomisé mirror. Together the surfaces evince the tobacco-filled pool halls of a bygone era. A multicolored chevron-patterned carpet establishes the color scheme for the other furnishings and draws your eyes from one side of the room to the other with its kinetic directional motif.”

## ANDREW BROWN

"In a small room such as this galley kitchen, a classic color scheme executed with a combination of textures, sheens, and patterns can impart movement and vitality. Here, black cocoons the space: there's black cerused oak on the faceted liquor cabinet, a black moiré wallcovering, black patent leather on the galley-style door, and black lacquer on the ceiling. Small brass accents create an atmosphere of masculine glamour, such as brass nailheads on the door, brass hardware on the cabinets, and jewellike brass light fixtures on the ceiling. Finally, black-and-white honed marble tiles on the floor and Calacatta Arabescato marble on the countertops add a little lightness and levity to the space, which might otherwise seem slightly claustrophobic."

GJELINA
FRANK STITT'S SOUTHERN TABLE

**GLENN GISSLER**

"This graciously scaled dining room in Greenwich Village had everything one might want in a proper dining room—but no window. That limitation became the germ of an idea. We commissioned artist Kevin Paulsen to paint a fantastical all-encompassing landscape mural where history meets contemporary imagination. The result is a room that offers more of a view than a mere window could ever provide."

**PATRICK MELE**

"This guest room on Cheyne Walk in London was meant to give the guests who inhabit it the ultimate escapist experience. It is hard to determine where the envelope of the room starts and ends in relation to the furnishings within it. All are clad in intricate patterns from a wide range of cultures. These motifs bounce and interact with one another, creating a dynamic push-pull that brings the room great energy and gusto!"

**PHILIP GORRIVAN**

"Mixing patterns—especially colorful, bold patterns—requires careful consideration. A strong visual narrative is key. In the case of this Park Avenue living room, the wallcovering, rug, and textiles are so balanced that one element would be lost without the other. Coral walls provide instant verve and excitement while complementing everyone's skin tone."

pierre cardin
DAVID HICKS

**PULP DESIGN STUDIOS**

Opposite: "We are known for bold and adventurous design, for rooms that are super dynamic but also livable, and that means thinking out of the box. In this office nook, we asked a muralist to create a stunning ceiling that would look as if the wallpaper pattern flew off the walls and escaped across the ceiling."

Overleaf: "It's the layering and the details that showcase the personality—or story—of the room. We layered chic and rich materials in this room, with muscovite, faux animal skins that mimic snake and shagreen, crystals, velvets, and more. Layering is key to really giving you that wonderful sense of opulence and drama.

Dior by Avedon
ANDY WARHOL
Polaroids 1958–1987
TASCHEN

DRUGS
NUDE

LUCINDA LOYA

Right: “These clients needed symmetry to feel most comfortable in their home, so to add interest we chose an irregular-edged rug to ground the room. The contrast makes a statement, and the royal blue adds an inviting jolt of color.”

Overleaf: “This historic home begged for decor that was full of personality, so we chose the most statement-making rug we could find, which did the trick. The vintage mirror was applied to the walls to bring life back into the room while referencing the age of the home. The glass affords a veiled reflection, as if the walls could talk.”

THE ART BOOK

THE BOOK OF TEA
MORE IS MORE

PIERCE & WARD

"Paint can be used in dramatic ways. Creating stripes is a trick we often utilize to make a big impact. Here the effect of these black-and-white stripes is enhanced by extending them up onto the ceiling and over all the nooks."

REDD KAIHOI

Opposite: "We like a balance of organic and graphic patterns. Here, the floor is painted to look like limestone with blue-green cabochons; it complements the walls, which feel like an organic fantasy garden. But it's the trompe l'oeil striped ceiling that somehow steals the show: it was the perfect foil to three skylights, and it makes this room feel like a conservatory in the sky."

Overleaf: "We sometimes find a great graphic stripe and use it all over the room. This zigzag stripe is a perfect example: it gives you a fantasy tent to dine in, which can be fun in a tropical atmosphere. The neutral-patterned floor covering provides a pitch-perfect balance, while the white elements in the space keep things fresh."

Special thanks to my literary agent, William Clark, who took a chance with me. This is our fourth book together, and I look forward to many more.

A word of thanks to everyone at Rizzoli New York, including publisher Charles Miers; my editor, Kathleen Jayes; my copy editor, Jennifer Milne; this book's designer, Susi Oberhelman; and my publicist, Jessica Napp.

A wealth of gratitude to my supportive friends and family. I am blessed. Thank you.

## SCHUMACHER

And a special word of thanks to Schumacher for providing all the background patterns in this book. It was a joy to work with Dara Caponigro and her team in choosing just the right patterns to help bring these pages to life. For your reference, here are the page numbers and patterns in the order they appear in the book.

Cover: Exotic Butterfly in Black
Endpapers: Pandora Embroidery in Aubergine
Reverse of Endpapers: Iconic Leopard in Fuchsia/Natural
Page 3: Primavera Stripe in Berry
Pages 14–15: Dawnridge in Peacock by Cristina Buckley
Pages 54–55: Idris Embroidery in Navy & Multi
Pages 94–95: Japura Forest in Green
Pages 134–135: Kashgar Velvet Ikat in Ruby & Plum
Pages 172–173: Shanghai Peacock in Cinnabar



ANDREW BROWN

"I love to add mirrors in rooms that are not perfectly proportioned from an architectural standpoint; it's a great way to trick the eye and visually expand the space. Using antiqued mirror is important, as it adds an element of age to a room—and creates a magical atmosphere at night with the mottled reflection of candlelight and chandeliers."

A WANDERING EYE
NEW YORK SPLENDOR
Wendy Moonan

# PHOTO CREDITS

Pages 2, 16, 18-19, 80, 81, 85, 90-91, 121, 128-129, 211, 212-213: © Eric Piasecki/OTTO

Pages 4-5, 38-39, 75, 76-77, 132, 133, 223: Stephen Karlisch

Page 7: Richard Powers

Pages 8-9, 24-25, 42-43, 96, 98-99, 162-163, 164-165: Annie Schlechter

Pages 11, 166-167, 219: Miguel Flores-Vianna/ The Interior Archive

Pages 12-13, 20-21, 79, 202-203: Chris Mottalini

Pages 146-147: Francesco Lagnese/Bunny Williams Interior Design

Pages 22-23, 72-73, 205: © Francesco Lagnese/ OTTO

Pages 26-27, 51, 220-221: Photography by Pieter Estersohn

Pages 28-29, 30-31, 92, 168-169, 183, 184-185, 232-233: Douglas Friedman/Trunk Archive

Pages 32-33: Lisa Pearson

Page 35: © William Waldron/OTTO

Pages 36-37, 100-101: Josh Thornton

Pages 40-41, 136, 143, 198-199, 201: Joshua McHugh

Pages 44-45: Brian Shumway

Pages 46-47, 190-191: George Ross Photographs

Pages 48-49: © Brittany Ambridge/OTTO (designed by Amanda Nisbet)

Pages 82-83: © Brittany Ambridge/OTTO

Pages 52-53, 58-59, 60-61, 159: © Stephen Kent Johnson/OTTO

Pages 56, 170-171: © Trevor Tondro/OTTO

Pages 63, 64-65: Photo by Reid Rolls/Bunny Williams Interior Design

Pages 66-67: Marius Chira/Instagram @marius.dof

Pages 68-69, 70-71, 122-123, 208-209: Photo by Reid Rolls

Pages 86-87, 192-193: Marco Ricca

Pages 88-89, 115: Tim Street-Porter

Pages 93, 127: Matthew Millman

Pages 102-103, 104-105: Image/Photo:Kris Tamburello

Pages 106-107: Nathan Rosenberg Photography

Pages 109, 124-125, 153, 196-197: Thomas Loof/ Trunk Archive

Pages 110-111: © Noe DeWitt/OTTO

Pages 112, 113, 116-117: Nelson Hancock

Pages 118-119, 150-151, 177, 178-179: Julie Soefer

Pages 131, 174: John Bessler

Pages 138-139: Dylan Chandler

Pages 140-141: STACY ZARIN GOLDBERG

Pages 144-145: Jonny Marlow

Pages 148-149, 214-215, 237: Hector M. Sanchez

Pages 154-155: Image copyright Read McKendree/JBSA

Pages 156-157: Laure Joliet

Pages 160-161: Simon Watson/Trunk Archive

Pages 180-181, 230: Nickolas Sargent

Pages 186-187: © Paul Costello/OTTO

Pages 188-189: Richard Leo Johnson/ Atlantic Archives Inc.

Page 195: Nathan Schroeder

Pages 206-207: Don Freeman

Pages 216-217: Photo by Gross & Daley

Pages 224-225: Cody Ulrich

Pages 226-227, 228-229: Giovanni Franchellucci

Pages 230-231: @Edward Badham

Pages 234-235: © Björn Wallander/OTTO (designed by Redd Kaihoi)

SASHA BIKOFF

"The mash-up of patterns developed throughout the space was inspired by the symbols of the iconic Memphis Milano movement from the 1980s. The color story references the art deco revival period on Miami Beach. The resulting staircase pays homage to the past while creating an artful installation, pushing the boundaries of maximalist design in a way that speaks to the millennial generation."

© Richard Koek

CARL DELLATORE began his career as a textile designer, and has worked extensively in magazines as well as textile design. He currently works as a content marketing consultant and social media strategist within New York's design community. He is the author of *The Fabric Style Book, Interior Design Master Class, On Style,* and *Garden Design Master Class.*

**PAGE 2**

**STEPHEN DIGERONIMO**

"It's important to trust your instincts when designing a maximalist space. Creating this New York City living room for public-relations maven Christina Juarez was a joy! She encouraged me to investigate an inventive color combination and to challenge myself in choosing design elements. The result is an interior that reflects her personality—colorful and energetic."

**PAGES 4–5**

**MICHELLE NUSSBAUMER**

"For this dynamic pattern-on-pattern 'writer's lair' for the Kips Bay Decorator Show House in Dallas, I conjured an imaginary nineteenth-century English novelist, who once lived in Morocco and Turkey, as my muse. The mix of compelling patterns in shades of blue and cream unify the space, while the archways reference distant locales."

First published in the United States of America in 2022 by
Rizzoli International Publications, Inc.
300 Park Avenue South
New York, NY 10010
www.rizzoliusa.com


Foreword: Dara Caponigro



Publisher: Charles Miers
Senior Editor: Kathleen Jayes
Design: Susi Oberhelman
Production Manager: Alyn Evans
Managing Editor: Lynn Scrabis



Printed in CHINA

2022 2023 2024 2025 / 10 9 8 7 6 5 4 3 2 1

ISBN: 978-0-8478-72374

Library of Congress Control Number: 2022932658

Visit us online:
Facebook.com/RizzoliNewYork
Twitter: @Rizzoli_Books
Instagram.com/RizzoliBooks
Pinterest.com/RizzoliBooks
Youtube.com/user/RizzoliNY
Issuu.com/Rizzoli

FSC
www.fsc.org
MIX
Paper | Supporting responsible forestry
FSC™ C007683

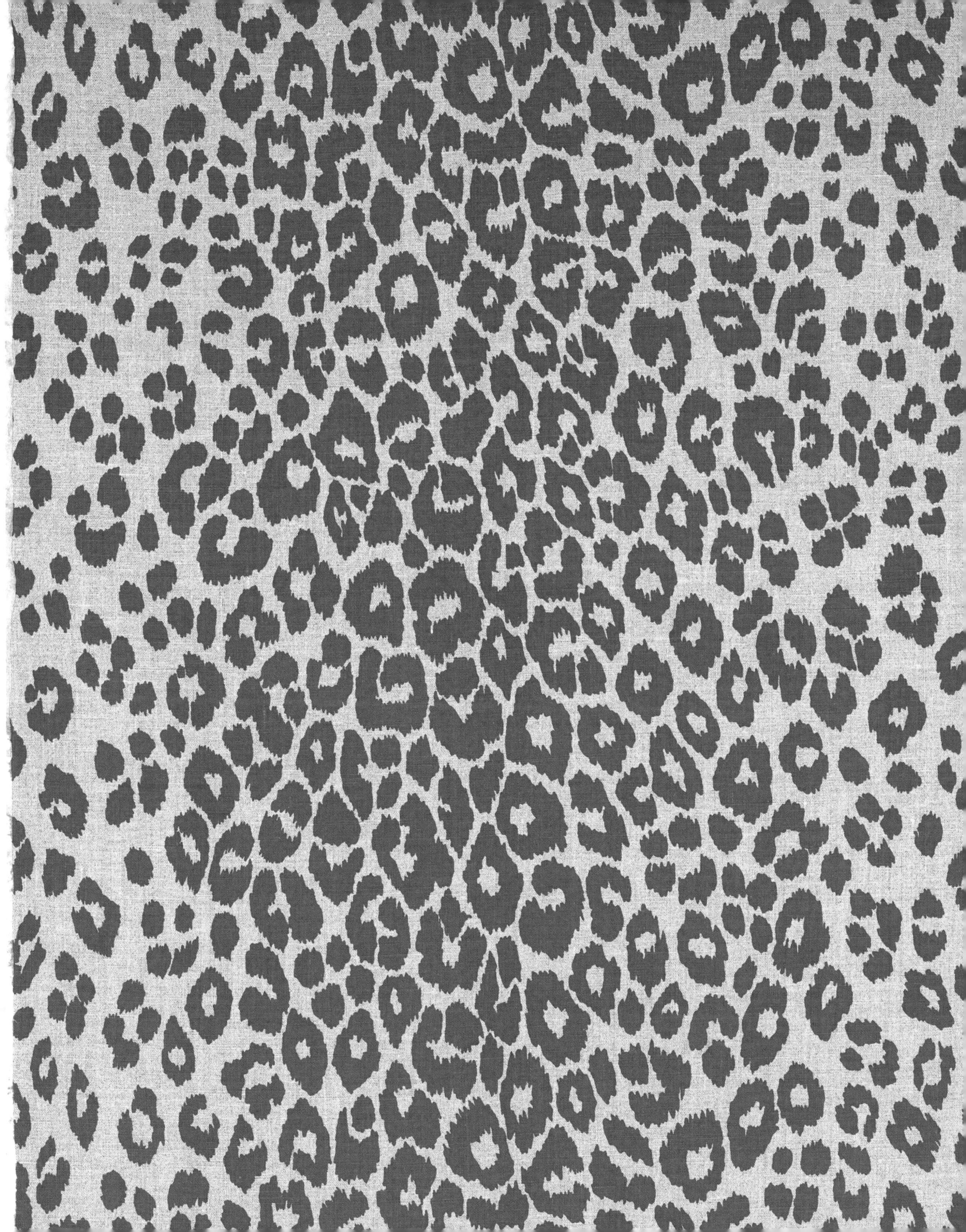